印を結び滝行をする阿含宗開祖・桐山靖雄

実践 輪廻転生瞑想法Ⅲ

あなたも仏陀になれる
水晶龍神瞑想法

阿含宗開祖
桐山靖雄

平河出版社

実践 輪廻転生瞑想法 III
あなたも仏陀になれる水晶龍神瞑想法
2017 年 2 月 1 日　第 1 版第 1 刷発行

著者　桐山靖雄

©2017 by Seiyu Kiriyama

発行者―森 眞智子

発行所―株式会社 平河出版社

〒 108-0073 東京都港区三田 3-4-8

電話 03(3454)4885 FAX.03(5484)1660

郵便振替 00110-4-117324

装幀―佐藤篤司

印刷所―凸版印刷 株式会社

用紙店―中庄 株式会社

Printed in Japan

落丁・乱丁本はお取り替えいたします。

本書の引用は自由ですが、必ず出版社の承諾を得ること。

ISBN978-4-89203-348-3 C0015

http://www.hirakawa-shuppan.co.jp

実践　輪廻転生瞑想法　Ⅲ

自分の思うように自分を変え、

自分の望むもの、願うことは、

かならず実現させずにはおかない、

そして、それは現世だけでなく、

来世さえも思うままに

つくり変える――、

そういう方法(システム)があったら、

どんなによいであろうかと

あなたは思わないか?

そういう方法(システム)があるならば、

ぜひとも学んで

自分の身につけたいものだと思わないか？

もちろん、思うのにちがいない。

そう思ったら、すぐに、

「輪廻転生瞑想法」をはじめることだ。

「輪廻転生瞑想法」をおこなえば、

だれでも──、

もちろん、あなただって、

思うままの人生をつくりだし、

理想の来世を迎えることができるのである。

仏説摩訶般若波羅蜜多心経

唐三蔵法師玄奘＝訳

観自在菩薩。行深般若波羅蜜多時。照見五蘊皆空。度一切苦厄。

舎利子。色不異空。空不異色。色即是空。空即是色。受想行識。

亦復如是。舎利子。是諸法空相。不生不滅。不垢不浄。不増不減。

是故空中。無色。無受想行識。無眼耳鼻舌身意。無色声香味触法。

無眼界。乃至無意識界。無無明。亦無無明尽。乃至無老死。

亦無老死尽。無苦集滅道。無智亦無得。以無所得故。菩提薩埵。

依般若波羅蜜多故。心無罣礙。無罣礙故。無有恐怖。

遠離（一切）顚倒夢想。究竟涅槃。三世諸仏。

依般若波羅蜜多故。得阿耨多羅三藐三菩提。故知般若波羅蜜多。

是大神呪。是大明呪。是無上呪。是無等等呪。能除一切苦。

真実不虚故。説般若波羅蜜多呪。即説呪曰。

掲帝。掲帝。般羅掲帝。般羅僧掲帝。菩提僧莎訶。

般若波羅蜜多心経。

准胝観音経

准胝功徳聚。寂静にして心常に誦すれば一切諸諸の大難能く是の人を侵すこと無し。天上及び人間福を受くること仏の如く等し。此の如意珠に遇はば定んで無等等を得ん。若し我れ誓願大悲の裡に一人として二世の願を成ぜずんば我れ虚妄罪過の裡に堕して本覚に帰らず大悲を捨てん。

準胝尊真言

ノウバ・サッタナン・サンミャクサンボダクチナン・タニャタ・オン・シャレ

イ・シュレイ・ジュンテイ・ソワカ

実践　輪廻転生瞑想法Ⅲ　目次

はじめに……… 14

高度の集中と瞑想の訓練法……… 19

シャマタとビバシャナ……… 20

さまざまなものをイメージする訓練……… 22

集中力を高める訓練……… 24

心をコントロールする訓練……… 26

成功を確信して努力する……… 28

花の瞑想法Ⅱ……… 31

花の瞑想法Ⅱ……… 32

四つのルートの訓練法……37

四つのルートの訓練法……38

[部類のルート]……38
グループ

[部分のルート]……40

[質のルート]……42

[経験のルート]……45

〈大輪の白いバラ〉を想起する……32

〈真紅のバラ〉を想起する……33

〈大輪の白いキク〉を想起する……33

〈オレンジ色のチューリップ〉を想起する……34

〈黄色いガーベラ〉を想起する……34

〈ピンクのボタン〉を想起する……34

〈青いアイリス〉を想起する……35

アージュニャー瞑想法……49

アージュニャー瞑想法……50

水晶龍神洗浄瞑想法……53

洗浄瞑想法……54

愛染明王秘密曼荼羅瞑想法……59

一—大虚空観……61

二—火天……62

三—倶利伽羅龍王……63

四―降三世明王………64

五―光明解脱輪宝………65

六―無能勝明王………69

七―如意宝幢………70

八―仏舎利尊………71

九―愛染明王………72

十―縁起観………73

十一―神霊（十二天）………74

瞑想を終える………75

はじめに

『実践輪廻転生瞑想法』は、瞑想者が「輪廻転生瞑想法」を、より明確に習得できるように映像化してDVDにおさめたものである。

『実践輪廻転生瞑想法』は三部構成となっている。

『実践輪廻転生瞑想法Ⅰ』では、「瞑想の基礎トレーニング」、瞑想の基本となる「花の瞑想法」、そして輪廻転生瞑想法のひとつである「如意宝珠敬愛法」を映像化した。

『実践輪廻転生瞑想法Ⅱ』では本格的な瞑想法に入る。交感神経を高める「火の呼吸法」、全身の気や血の流れを盛んにする「意念（こころ）の訓練」、驚異的効力を得る「クンダリニー・パールの授与」「チャクラ開発」「スヴァーディシュターナ瞑想法」、よりいっそう仏陀に近づく「輪廻転生曼荼羅瞑想法」を映像化した。

そして最後の『実践輪廻転生瞑想法Ⅲ』では、さらに高度な瞑想法を実践するための「高

度の集中と瞑想の訓練法」、瞑想の基本第二弾「花の瞑想法Ⅱ」、想起と集中を同時におこなう「四つのルートの訓練法」、魔法のクンダリニー・パールをもちいてホルモンを思うように分泌させる「アージュニャー瞑想法」、水晶を使って深層意識を活用する「水晶龍神洗浄瞑想法」、最後に「愛染明王秘密曼荼羅瞑想法」を映像化してある。

本来、これまで教えてきた訓練法は、筆や映像にすべきではないとされている。なぜならば、脳のチャクラの訓練は、修行のしかたによっては危険であり、慎重にしなければならないからである。

困難な訓練法を、安心して修行できるよう、わかりやすく映像化したので、これらの瞑想法をしっかりと身につけていただきたい。

「輪廻転生瞑想法」を映像化したテキストは、この『実践輪廻転生瞑想法Ⅲ』をもってひとまず完結する。

熱心な修行者のために、可能な範囲で解説し映像化したが、「輪廻転生瞑想法」には、

まだまだ先がある。奥が深いのである。

これ以上の段階の訓練を望む場合も、そうでない場合も、まず、本書の内容を、しっかりと修行した上で、わたくしか、わたくしの直接の指導を受けた弟子のもとで、訓練を受けることをお勧めする。

最後に、最も大切な心構えを伝えておく。

輪廻転生から脱することを説かれた仏陀釈尊のことを「万徳円満」という。すべての徳が完全にそなわっている、というのである。

徳なくして仏陀になれるはずがない。わかりきったことである。

不徳で、不運の者は、なにをしても成就しないのである。

「輪廻転生瞑想法」もそうである。

「輪廻転生瞑想法」の一面は〝技術〟である。しかしまた、〝技術〟だけでは「輪廻転生瞑想法」は成就できない。修行に耐えられるだけの〝徳〟と〝運〟のない人は、いくら「輪廻転生瞑想法」を修行しても達成できない。

いや、技術を習得すること自体ができないのである。かならず、障害が生じ、修行をつづけることができなくなる。あるいは、自ら力尽き、落伍し、行を廃絶する。

できるかぎり徳を積んで、自分を高めることである。

この心構えで、「輪廻転生瞑想法」を実践するならば、かならず、よりよい未来、理想的な来世を迎えることができるのである。

二〇一六年六月吉日

著者しるす

現世にて成道を果たされた阿含宗開祖・桐山靖雄大僧正は、二〇一六年八月二十九日に仏界へと赴かれました。仏陀として永遠の生命を得られた開祖は、これまでよりも一層強いお力で、「輪廻転生瞑想法」の実践に励む者、真の仏道を歩む者を守護してくださることでしょう。──阿含宗教学部

高度の集中と瞑想の訓練法

シャマタとビバシャナ

瞑想というのは、心を使う訓練である。心の使い方、心の能力といってもいいが、その心の能力の訓練には二つある。

まず一つは集中するということ、つぎに拡大するということ、この二つである。

これはサンスクリット語で、シャマタとヴィパシュヤナー（漢音写でシャマタとビバシャナ）という。

このシャマタとビバシャナを中国の僧侶がじつに簡単明瞭に、シャマタを「止」、ビバシャナを「観」と漢訳した。そして天台宗を開いた天台大師智顗が体系化した。これは非常に名訳である。

要するに止というのは、心を集中し一点にとどめる。心を集中していく。たとえば最初は花全体を見ている。ずーっと見ているうちに、集中してこの花の中心に心をとどめて動かさない。これがほんとうの集中力である。

心の使い方で、集中力というものは非常に大切なものである。強い集中力、まずこれを養わなければいけない。

しかし集中だけではだめである。観というものもある。

観というのは、心の中で映像を観るのである。心の中でひとつの映像、イメージを描いてこれを観る。

止というのは、いうならば、そのイメージに心を集中して動かさない。

観は、観ずるということで、密教では観想ともいう。

想というのは映像だと思えばいい。映像、イメージである。はっきりとイメージを持つ。そのイメージを描くだけではだめである。イメージを観るのである。だから、観、想と二つある。

イメージをして、イメージを持ったうえで、それを観る。強く観る。深く観察するという観方。そして、観たものに心を集中してとどめる。だから、止と観は別々ではない。ひとつなのである。

さまざまなものをイメージする訓練

心の中でさまざまなものをイメージする。それはただ単にイメージするだけではない。

自分の修行に必要なものをイメージして、イメージしたものに心を集中する。そして、そ

れに心をとどめて、そのイメージを動かさない。動かさないで、それに集中し、そのイ

メージに強く心を向けていく。

じつは、それよりもっとさきの修行もあるが、いまは、これだけでも精いっぱいでそ

こまで行かないので、まずは、とどめる練習、修行をしなければいけない。

そこで、なにをイメージするかということが問題になる。なにをイメージするか、そ

れはグルがあたえる。

グルは、最初のうちはみんなにおなじものをイメージの素材としてあたえるが、そのうち、

年齢や体質とかいった点からいろいろちがったものをあたえるようになる。

たとえば、丸いものをイメージしなさいといっても、ある人はお団子をイメージする

かもしれないし、お月さまをイメージするかもしれない。またある人は、家にあるお盆を

イメージするかもしれない。それは人によってみなちがう。

そういうように、こういうイメージを持ちなさいということをグルはひとつひとつ教えていく。

そして、そのイメージに心を集中しなさいと教える。

この二つの能力、シャマタとビバシャナは、どんどん修行していくと、その集中力によって自分自身の体の細胞まで動かすことができるようになる。

たとえば自分の胃に心を集中する。そうすると、その集中によって、胃液の分泌をさせることができる。

喉（のど）が渇いたときに、梅干しなどを想像すると、つばが湧いてくる。

昔、三国志に出てくる有名な曹操という人が兵隊を率いて行軍していたら、水がなくなってしまい、みな喉が渇いて倒れそうになった。

そのとき、ずーっと向こうのほうに林が見えて、曹操がみなに「あれは梅の林だ、梅林なんだ。あそこへ行くと、いま、青梅がたくさんなっているから、行ってあれを食べたら喉の渇きがなくなるぞ」といった。

梅と聞いた途端にみなつばが出てきた。からからの口の中につばが出てきて、それで渇きをしのいだ。しかし、行ってみたら梅林じゃない、なにかの林だったが、一時の喉の渇きがそれで止められたという。

これがイメージなのである。

集中力を高める訓練

さらに今後、その集中力を高めるために、漠然とものを見るということはやめ、つねに注意を集めてものを観る。

おなじ見るにしても、この「観る」で観なければならない。見物の「見」ではだめである。ただじろじろ視るだけでもだめ。観察という観方、それが習慣になってくると、ぱっと観ただけでも、頭の中にぱーんと焼きつくようになる。ただぱっと観て、こちらを観て、あちらを観て、それをそのまま眼の中で描くことができる。そこまでやらなければならない。

わたくしが若いころ、観る力、ビバシャナとシャマタの力を養うためにいろいろな修

行をした。

たとえば、本を読んでいるとき、疲れて外を見る。そうすると、電線があって、そこに鳥が何羽かとまっている。

その鳥をぱっと観てすぐ眼をつぶる。そして、それを眼の中で再現して、眼の中に残っている鳥を数える。眼の中にその鳥が映っているから、一羽、二羽、三羽、四羽、五羽、六羽、こっちのほうに一羽、二羽……、合計十六羽とか、そのぐらいはだれでもすぐにできるようになる。

これが三十五、六羽ぐらいになるとこんがらがってしまう。

上の段には何羽だったかなどと考えてはいけない。考えるのはだめである。

考えないで、観たものをそのまま観る。

眼の前にあるふすまをぱっと観て、一枚、二枚、三枚、四枚、五枚、六枚、七枚と数える。

人の顔をぱっと観て、真ん中に鼻があって、眼が上にあって……、そういう観察力を養うことがシャマタ、ビバシャナの訓練になっていく。

実践　輪廻転生瞑想法Ⅲ

本を観る、読まない……。観て、眼をつぶって、出てくる文字をたどっていく……。

若いとき、そういう訓練をずいぶんした。

こういう訓練はいつでもできるのである。

通勤、通学の電車の中で、つり革にぶらさがっているとき、ずーっと向こうにビルが

あらわれる。ぱっと眼をつぶって、そのビルの窓を数えるのである。こちら側の窓はこう、

あちら側の窓はこうとか考えてはだめである。考えないで、ぱっと観て、眼をつぶって、

眼の中に残っているものを数える。

一カ月ぐらいやるとずいぶんちがってくる。

ただ眼で観て数える。それもひとつの方法だが、もっと心を自分の思うように使う方

法を身につけなければいけない。

心をコントロールする訓練

心を使うにはどうしたらいいか、どういう方法があるのか、それは呼吸である。

人間は息をしている。だれでも息をしている。この呼吸する息と心とは一体なのである。

心と呼吸はきわめて密接な関係にある。

心はなかなか自分の思うようにはならないが、呼吸はある程度自分の思うようになる。

だから、心と呼吸が密接な関係にあり一体であるのならば、呼吸をコントロールすることにより、心をコントロールすることができるようになるというわけである。

心だけをコントロールしようとしても、なかなかうまくいかない。

ぱっと観て、ぱっと注意力を高めて、それを数えるのもひとつの方法であるが、それは根本的なものではない。

根本的に心を自由にコントロールし、心を自由に使うようにするにはどうしたらいいか。それには、まず、呼吸をコントロールするところから入っていく。なぜならば、心をコントロールするということはむずかしいが、呼吸をコントロールすることはそうむずかしくないからである。深呼吸をしなさい。ふーっ、すーっとすぐできる。もっと速く呼吸する、止める。これはすぐできる。

呼吸から入っていって、そして心をコントロールできるようにしていくということである。

実践 輪廻転生瞑想法Ⅲ

成功を確信して努力する

これから、瞑想法をしっかり学ぶにあたっての心構えをのべる。

それは成功を確信して努力していくということである。そうすると、成功するためのいろいろな知恵が出てくる。それなのに、おれはだめだ、もうだめだと思ったら知恵がはたらかなくなってくる。だめなものには知恵のはたらきようがない。だめだと自分でストップをかけていてはなんの進歩もない。

おれは絶対成功するぞ、そう思っていると成功するための知恵がはたらいてくる。それで、かならず成功する。

愚痴、泣き言、人の批判、人のかげ口は絶対にだめである。それは自分の徳を損ずる。かげ口や悪口をいっているときの顔というのは卑しいものである。ずっと人のかげ口や悪口ばかりいっていると、人は卑しい顔になってくる。

人間というのは、明るく、人の悪口をいわない。そういう明るい人柄を人は好むものである。

28

人柄がよくならなければ、だれも応援しない。好意を持ってくれない。人に好意を持っ

てもらえないようでは大きい仕事はできないのである。

大きい仕事をしている人は、みなにかならず好意を持ってもらい、あの人だったら協

力しよう、あの人のためだったらという気持ちにさせる。

その反対に人柄が悪いと、あいつがやるんだったらと足を引っ張る、あいつがやるん

だったらただじゃおかない、となる。どんなに偉い人でも人柄が悪いとうまくいかない。

よい人柄をつくるためには、心が明るくなければいけない。それには絶対マイナスの

言葉を使わない。人のかげ口をいわない。暗いことは考えない。

いつも明るく、明朗に行動していく。明朗な考え方をする。そうすると、一カ月もた

つと顔が変わってくる。そういうふうにならなければいけない。

修行をつづけていると潜在意識の力が非常に強くなるので、つねに自分をよいほうへ、

よいほうへと暗示をかけていく。するとそのとおりの人間になっていくのである。

だから、今日からマイナスの言葉は使わない。絶対に成功するという確信を持ってこ

の瞑想をつづけていくことである。

花の瞑想法II

花の瞑想法をはじめる。

花からはじめるのは、花のように清らかな美しい心を持つことが、瞑想の大きな目的のひとつだからである。

花の瞑想法Ⅱ

これからおこなうのは、「想起」と「集中」を同時におこなう瞑想法である。

半跏趺坐でゆったりと座る。

どうしてもできない人は、椅子に掛けてもかまわない。

まず、ゆっくりと息を吐く。

そのあと、ゆっくりと吸う。

静かに呼吸をしよう。

〈大輪の白いバラ〉を想起する

呼吸と心が調ったら、眼を閉じて一輪の大きな白いバラを想おう。

その白いバラを心の中心に置く。

そして、白いバラを凝視する。

白いバラという概念ではなく、ほんとうに白いバラそのものを想い起こす。

〈真紅のバラ〉を想起する

つぎに、白いバラをそのまま心にとめておきながら、真紅のバラを想い起こす。

真紅のバラという概念ではなく、ほんとうの真紅のバラそのものである。

そのバラの赤い色をしっかりと想い起こす。

赤い色という概念ではなく、赤い色そのものである。

しかし、中心に置いた白いバラを忘れてはいけない。

〈大輪の白いキク〉を想起する

つぎに、白いバラをそのまま心にとめておきながら、白い大輪のキクを想い起こす。

真紅のバラは消してもかまわない。

実践 輪廻転生瞑想法 Ⅲ

白い大輪のキクという概念ではなく、ほんとうの白い大輪のキクそのものである。

その大輪のキクの白い色をしっかりと想い起こす。

白い色という概念ではなく、白い色そのものである。

しかし、中心に置いた白いバラを忘れてはいけない。

〈オレンジ色のチューリップ〉を想起する

つぎに、白いバラをそのまま心にとめておきながら、オレンジ色のチューリップを想い起こす。

〈黄色いガーベラ〉を想起する

つぎに、白いバラをそのまま心にとめておきながら、黄色いガーベラを想い起こす。

〈ピンクのボタン〉を想起する

つぎに、白いバラをそのまま心にとめておきながら、ピンクのボタンを想い起こす。

34

〈青いアイリス〉を想起する

つぎに、白いバラをそのまま心にとめておきながら、青いアイリスを想い起こす。

最後に青いアイリスを消して花の瞑想を終わる。

いまは白いバラを中心に置いたが、固定する花は随時、変えてもかまわない。

最も大切なことは、決して概念ではなく、おのおのの花のかたちや色を鮮明に想い起こすことである。

この瞑想法は、心をひとつのことに固定すると同時に、一方で、その固定したものに関連したものをつぎつぎと想い起こしていく。

「想起」と「集中」の二つを同時におこなうことで、脳のはたらきをとても高めてくれる。

四つのルートの訓練法

「想起」と「集中」をしっかりおこなうためには、中心課題の発展のさせ方を工夫しなければならない。

そのために必要な、思念の四つのルートを訓練していこう。

四つのルートの訓練法

訓練前の心得として、まず、呼吸を乱さないように、随息観……、つまり、息を数えず自然に任せるような呼吸を心掛ける。

そして、ひとつの具体的な対象を定め、それを注意深く心の中に置く。

そこから離れず、その対象を四つの思念のルートに乗せて、自由に思考をはたらかせる。

むやみに緊張してはいけない。

時間を合わせるために時計を見るように、心静かに臨む……。それがコツである。

[部類のルート]

まず最初の訓練は「部類のルート」である。

ここでは、牧場を舞台にして、そこで暮らす〈牛〉という動物を例にとって訓練していこう。牛に類似する動物を想起していく。

〈牛〉

ゆっくりと眼を閉じ、まず一頭の牛を想い起こす。

牛という概念ではなく、牛そのものである。

この牛を想いの中心に置きながら、おなじ部類の動物を考える。

〈羊〉

たとえば、ここでは羊を想い起こす。

あくまでも、牛を想いの中心に置きながら、まず羊をしっかりと想い起こす。

羊という概念ではなく、羊そのものである。

実践　輪廻転生瞑想法Ⅲ

〈馬〉

そのつぎは、馬を想い起こす。

羊は消してもかまわない。

あくまでも、牛を想いの中心に置きながら、馬をしっかりと想い起こす。

〈犬〉

そのつぎは、犬を想い起こす。

馬は消してもかまわない。

あくまでも、牛を想いの中心に置きながら、犬をしっかりと想い起こす。

このように、牛に類似する動物を想起していく。

[**部分のルート**]

二つめの訓練は「部分のルート」である。

40

牛の体を構成する、さまざまな「部分」を想起していく。

ゆっくりと眼を閉じ、ふたたび一頭の牛を想い起こす。

この牛を想いの中心に置きながら、牛のさまざまな「部分」を考える。

〈牛の耳〉

たとえば、ここでは牛の耳を想い起こす。

あくまでも、一頭の牛を想いの中心に置きながら、まず牛の耳をしっかりと想い起こす。

牛の耳という概念ではなく、牛の耳そのものである。

これは牛の「部分」であると考える。

〈牛の鼻〉

そのつぎは、牛の鼻を想い起こす。

牛の耳は消してもかまわない。

あくまでも、一頭の牛を想いの中心に置きながら、牛の鼻をしっかりと想い起こす。

実践 輪廻転生瞑想法III

牛の鼻という概念ではなく、牛の鼻そのものである。

〈牛のひづめ〉

そのつぎは、牛のひづめを想い起こす。

牛の鼻は消してもかまわない。

あくまでも、一頭の牛を想いの中心に置きながら、牛のひづめをしっかりと想い起こす。

牛のひづめという概念ではなく、牛のひづめそのものである。

このように、牛の体を構成するさまざまな部分を想起していく。

［質のルート］

三つめの訓練は「質のルート」である。

牛の色やかたち、大きさ、仕草など、さまざまな「性質」を想起していく。

ゆっくりと眼を閉じ、ふたたび一頭の牛を想い起こす。

42

この牛を想いの中心に置きながら、まずは牛の動きについて考える。

あくまでも、一頭の牛を想いの中心に置きながら、牛の動きをしっかりと想い起こす。

〈カメ〉

ゆっくりとした動き、それはまるで、カメである。

カメという概念ではなく、カメそのものを想い起こす。

これは牛の動きとおなじようにゆっくりとしたカメであると考える。

〈トラクター〉

つぎは、牛の大きさについて考える。

牛とおなじように大きくて力強く、堂々としたもの。

それはトラクターである。

カメは消してもかまわない。

あくまでも、一頭の牛を想いの中心に置きながら、トラクターをしっかりと想い起こす。

トラクターという概念ではなく、トラクターそのものである。

これは牛とおなじように大きなトラクターであると考える。

〈碁石〉

今度は、牛の色について考える。

乳牛とおなじような白黒の色。

それは、囲碁などに使われる碁石である。

トラクターは消してもかまわない。

あくまでも、一頭の牛を想いの中心に置きながら、碁石をしっかりと想い起こす。

碁石という概念ではなく、碁石そのものである。

これは牛とおなじような色の、碁石であると考える。

このように、牛の色やかたち、大きさ、仕草などさまざまな性質を想起していく。

[経験のルート]

最後の四つめの訓練は「経験のルート」である。

あなたが〈牛〉から連想するさまざまなもの、「経験」によって印象づけられた事象を想起していく。

ゆっくりと眼を閉じ、ふたたび一頭の牛を想い起こす。

この牛を想いの中心に置きながら、あなたの心に印象づけられている牛を想い起こす。

牛から連想する、さまざまなイメージのひろがりを想い起こす。

〈ミルク〉

ここではミルクを想い起こす。

あくまでも、一頭の牛を想いの中心に置きながら、まずは牛からとれるミルクをしっかりと想い起こす。

ミルクという概念ではなく、ミルクそのものである。

これは牛からとれるミルクであると考える。

〈牛舎〉

つぎは、牛が暮らす牧場の牛舎を想い起こす。

ミルクは消してもかまわない。

あくまでも、一頭の牛を想いの中心に置きながら、牛舎という概念ではなく、牛舎そのものである。

これは牛が暮らす牧場の牛舎であると考える。

〈牧草〉

つぎは、牛が食べる牧草を想い起こす。

牛舎は消してもかまわない。

あくまでも、一頭の牛を想いの中心に置きながら、牧草をしっかりと想い起こす。

牧草という概念ではなく、牧草そのものである。

これは牛が食べる牧草であると考える。

このように、あなたが〈牛〉から連想するさまざまなもの、「体験」によって印象づけられた事柄を想起していく。

この訓練がもたらす利益は、じつに多くのはかりしれないものがある。

心がぼんやりと放浪して歩く悪い習慣を直し、長いあいだ、ひとつのことに注意を集中し、持続させる力をつけてくれる。

心の照準をひとつのものに定め、思いや想像を遊ばせるということは、潜在意識の活用に欠かすことができない。

さらに訓練を積むと、深層意識を動かすコツがわかってくる。

短い時間でもかまわないので、かならず毎日おこなうようにしよう。

アージュニャー瞑想法

「アージュニャー瞑想法」は、魔法のクンダリニー・パールをもちいて、自分が必要とするホルモンを思うように分泌し、湧き出させることができる瞑想法である。

そのホルモンは、あなたに魔法のように驚異的な力をあたえてくれることだろう。

ここでは、アージュニャー・チャクラの開発法をおこなう。

アージュニャー瞑想法

結跏趺坐、または半跏趺坐で、ゆったりと座る。

どうしてもできない人は、椅子に掛けてもかまわない。

火の呼吸法ができる人は、最初におこなう。

そして、長出入息呼吸法をおよそ二分間おこなう。

つぎに、長出息呼吸法をおよそ五分間おこなう。

反式呼吸ができる人は、反式呼吸法をおこなう。

（ただし、妊娠している人、もしくは、その可能性のある人は反式呼吸法は控える）

そして、観想——すなわち、これからおこなうことへ想いを馳せ、心を集中させよう。

導師からいただいたクンダリニー・パールを口の中に含む。

口に含んだパールを齦交に置く。

そして、舌の下から、チャクラ・プラーナ・ルートに入れる。

そして、舌の先から、パールを齦交に移す。

長出息法の呼吸に乗せて、パールをしだいに下の方へ移動させていく。

承漿から瞳中へ……。

瞳中から神闕へ……。

そして、神闕から、男性なら気海、女性なら関元まで、徐々に移動させる。

長出息呼吸法を十〜十五回位おこなう間に、パールを気海、関元まで到達させる。

気海、あるいは関元に到達すると、パールは、およそ二倍の大きさに膨張し、しだいに光を放ち、輝きはじめる。

ここで、およそ五〜十回、長出息呼吸法をおこなう。

しだいに、パールは輝きをおさめ、もとの大きさに戻る。

やがて、パールは、上昇しはじめる。

およそ十〜十五回の呼吸で、パールはもとの齦交に戻る。

齦交に到達したパールは、そのまま督脈ルートに入り、さらに上昇をつづける。

そして、兌端、水溝、素髎、神庭を通過する。

前頂と百会の中間に達したパールは、そこから脳の中心に向かって進入していく。

やがてパールは下垂体に到達し、アージュニャー・チャクラに到達する。

アージュニャー・チャクラにとどまったパールは、およそ二倍の大きさに膨張し、し

だいに光を放ち、輝きはじめる。

このときの呼吸の回数は、あなたの思いのままおこなう。

やがて、パールは輝きをおさめ、もとの大きさに戻る。

呼吸法に乗って、パールはいま通ってきたチャクラ・プラーナ・ルートをたどって、

もとの齦交に戻る。

パールが齦交に戻ったら、長出息呼吸法をおよそ十回。

呼吸を調える。

ゆっくり、立つ。

水晶龍神洗浄瞑想法

この瞑想法は、水晶を使って深層意識を活用する瞑想法である。

まずは、水晶を準備しよう。

穢れのない天然の水晶が理想である。

その水晶の中に意識を集中する。

水晶の中を凝視していると、モヤモヤとしたさまざまなものが見えてくる。

さらに心を静めて凝視していると、やがて龍神のお姿が見えてくる。

このお姿がはっきりと見えてくるようにならなくてはいけない。

モヤモヤの中にお顔やお体が見えてくるには三日ほどかかる。

観想も、このお姿をよく観察して瞑想しなくてはならない。

洗浄瞑想法

まずは、心身を浄める「洗浄瞑想法」から入る。

龍神に雨を降らしていただき、その龍雨によって、

心身の不浄不快がすべて洗い流され、病気の根もすべて洗い流される。

目の前に穢れのない水晶を置く。

水晶を見つめていると、やがて変化が起こる。

澄み渡った青空に突然一塊の雲が沸き起こる。

そして、一陣の風も吹きはじめた。

たちまち空一面、黒い雲に覆われてしまう。

さらに風は、激しく吹き荒れる。

その黒い雲の中心に金色の龍王を想い、心を集中させる。

この龍王は、水晶で見ているお姿である。

金色の龍王が、大神通力をもって暴風を起こしているのである。

さらに、大雨が降ってきた。

滝のように降ってくる大雨を頭から受ける。

それは、あたかも滝行のようである。

この大雨によって、心身の不浄不快が、悉く洗い流されていく。

病気の根もすべて洗い流してくれる。

そう想いを馳せて、　般若心経を五回唱える。

つぎに想いを馳せ、

「わが心身爽快なり。　わが身の不浄不快悉く消滅す」

と念じる。

そして、準胝真言を五回唱えてよびかける。

「オン・シャレイ・シュレイ・ジュンテイ・ソワカ」

最後に、

「臨兵闘者皆陳列在前、エイッ」

と九字を三回切って終わる。

毎朝一回、十五分ほどかけてこの瞑想をおこなう。

この洗浄瞑想法を毎日重ねて実行していると、一日中体が元気で爽快になり、さらに

龍神にご守護いただけるようになる。

愛染明王秘密曼荼羅瞑想法

●瞑想に入る前に、『実践輪廻転生瞑想法Ⅰ』「瞑想の準備」以下をすませておくこと。

一 大虚空観

果てしなき大虚空を想え。
太陽系・銀河系を遙か彼方に。
その中心に身を置き、坐せ。

二 ― 火天(かてん)

わが眼前に 𑖨 (ラン)字あり。
𑖨 (ラン)字変じて火天となり、
大火炎を起こす。
大火炎、護摩の炎となって
虚空中に遍満す。

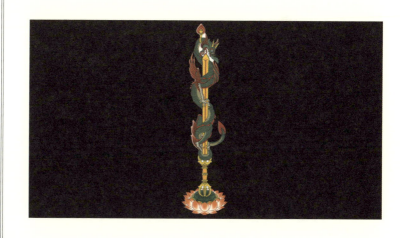

三——倶利伽羅龍王

護摩の大火炎の中に倶利伽羅龍王出現す。
変じて不動明王となる。
自身、護摩の炎と一体になると想え。

ノウマク・サンマンダ・バザラダン・カン。

四──降三世明王

大火炎の中に（ウン）字あり。
降三世明王となる。
この尊の火光、自身の心を照らし、
悪縁を呼び込む三毒の心、
貪・瞋・癡を降伏す。

オン・ソンバ・ニソンバ・ウン・バザラ・ウン・ハッタ。

五―光明解脱輪宝(こうみょうげだつりんぼう)

火光の中に
光明解脱輪宝出現す。
輪宝、自身の臍輪に安置せよ。
火炎を発して、
わが全身を包み込む。

実践 輪廻転生瞑想法Ⅲ

輪宝、自身の額に安置せよ。
火炎を発して自身の身業を焼き尽くす。

Practicing
Meditation
for Reincarnation
Part III
How to Achieve Nirvana through
Crystal Dragon God Meditation
Seiyu Kiriyama
Founder of Agon Shu Buddhist Association

HIRAKAWA SHUPPAN

Seiyu Kiriyama
Founder of Agon Shu Buddhist Association,
Practicing Meditation under a Waterfall

Practicing
Meditation
for Reincarnation
(Part III)

How to Achieve Nirvana through
Crystal Dragon God Meditation

Seiyu Kiriyama

Founder of Agon Shu Buddhist Association

HIRAKAWA SHUPPAN INC.

Copyright ©2017 by Seiyu Kiriyama
All rights reserved. No part of this publication may be reproduced
without prior permission in writing from the publisher.

First published in 2017 by
HIRAKAWA SHUPPAN INC.
Mita 3-4-8, Minato-ku, Tokyo 108-0073, Japan

Designed by Atsushi Sato
Printed and bound in Japan by TOPPAN Printing Co., Ltd.
Paper supplied by NAKASHO, Inc.

We must strive to transform ourselves into who we want to be and to make our dreams come true.

Moreover, wouldn't it be great if there were a way to change yourself not only in this life but in your next life as well?

Haven't you ever thought of how great it would be if such a way existed?

If there were such a way, wouldn't you certainly want to learn and master it?

If you feel this way, then you should start Meditation for Reincarnation immediately.

If you, or anyone, practices Meditation for Reincarnation, you will be able to lead a satisfying life as well as create an ideal next life.

The Heart Sutra
(*Bussetsu Maka Hannya Haramita Shingyo*)

Translated by the monk Hsüan-tsang (Xuanzang, 600-664)
of the T'ang Dynasty from Sanskrit into Chinese.

Japanese Reading

Kanjizai Bosatsu
Gyo Jin Hannya Haramita Ji
Shoken Go'un Kai Ku
Do Issai Kuyaku
Sharishi
Shiki Fu I Ku
Ku Fu I Shiki
Shiki Soku Ze Ku
Ku Soku Ze Shiki
Ju So Gyo Shiki Yaku Bu Nyoze
Sharishi
Ze Shoho Kuso
Fusho Fumetsu
Fuku Fujo
Fuzo Fugen
Ze Ko Ku Chu
Mu Shiki
Mu Ju So Gyo Shiki
Mu Gen Ni Bi Zetsu Shin Ni
Mu Shiki Sho Ko Mi Soku Ho
Mu Genkai
Naishi Mu Ishikikai
Mu Mumyo
Yaku Mu Mumyo Jin
Naishi Mu Roshi

Yaku Mu Roshi Jin
Mu Ku Ju Metsu Do
Mu Chi Yaku Mu Toku
I Mu Shotoku Ko
Bodaisatta
E Hannya Haramita Ko
Shin Mu Keige
Mu Keige Ko
Mu U Kufu
Onri Issai Tendo Muso
Kugyo Nehan
Sanze Shobutsu
E Hannya Haramita Ko
Toku Anokutara Sanmyaku Sanbodai
Ko Chi Hannya Haramita
Ze Dai Jinshu
Ze Dai Myoshu
Ze Mujoshu
Ze Mu Todoshu
No Jo Issai Ku
Shinjitu Fu Ko Ko
Setsu Hannya Haramita Shu
Soku Setsu Shu Watsu
Gyatei
Gyatei
Haragyatei
Harasogyatei
Boji Sowaka

Hannya Haramita Shingyo

The Cundi Avalokiteshvara Sutra
(*Juntei Kannon-Kyo*)

In the presence of Cundi,[1] accumulate merit.

Be free from all worldly thoughts while reciting this mantra,
receive great merit in Cundi, and elude all manner of misfortune.

All sentient beings of heavenly and human realms
shall be blessed with virtues as attained by a Buddha.

For in knowing Cundi,
the Wish-Fulfilling Jewel lies within one's grasp.

With complete and wholehearted faith in Cundi,
all shall be saved both in this life and in the next.
Yet should even a single soul be denied such liberation,
then shall I be damned for the sin of deception,
and my path shall part from the way of the Buddha,
as I suffer the sins of hell.

The Cundi Mantra (*Junteison Shingon*)

NOBA SATTANAN SAN-MYAKU-SANBODA-KUCHINAN
TANYATA ON SHAREI SHUREI JUNTEI SOWAKA

---

[1] Cundi: pronounced 'Chundi'.

Contents

Prologue.........11

Methods for Practicing Deep Concentration and Meditation.........15

Shamatha and Vipashyana.........16
Methods for Visualizing All Sorts of
    Objects in Your Mind.........17
Training to Enhance the Ability to Concentrate.........19
Training to Control the Mind.........20
Strive, Sure of Success.........21

Flower Meditation Method II.........25

Flower Meditation Method II.........26
    Visualize a White Rose.........26
    Visualize a Red Rose.........26
    Visualize a White Chrysanthemum.........26
    Visualize an Orange Tulip.........27
    Visualize a Yellow Daisy.........27

Visualize a Pink Peony.........27

Visualize a Blue Iris.........27

How to Practice the Four Routes.........29

How to Practice the Four Routes.........30

The Group Route.........30

The Parts Route.........31

The Quality Route.........32

The Experience Route.........33

Ajna Meditation Method.........37

Ajna Meditation Method.........38

Crystal Dragon God Cleansing and Meditation Method.........41

Cleansing Meditation Method.........42

Ragaraja Secret Mandala Meditation Method.........45

1. Visualize a Vast Sky.........46

2. Agni.........47

3. Dragon God Kulika.........48

4. Trailokyavijaya.........49

5. Chakraratna.........50

6. Aparajita.........54

7. Wish-Fulfilling Banner.........55

8. Sacred Relics of the Buddha.........56

9. Ragaraja.........57

10. Contemplation of Dependent Arising.........58

11. Twelve Gods.........59

Concluding the Meditation.........60

Prologue

Practicing Meditation for Reincarnation contains the text of the accompanying videos on Meditation for Reincarnation, which are intended to clarify and facilitate the meditator's learning of this meditation technique.

Practicing Meditation for Reincarnation is composed of three parts.

Part I provides visual explanations of the basics of meditation, the Flower Meditation (which is the basis of meditation), and the Secret Wish-Fulfilling Jewel Dharma of Reverence and Love, which is one of the meditation techniques for reincarnation.

Part II describes full-fledged meditation techniques, and the video provides visual explanations of the Breath of Fire, which stimulates the sympathetic nervous system; Mind Training, which invigorates the flow of qi and blood through the body; Confering of the Kundalini Pearl, Awakening of the Chakras, and Svadhishthana Meditation, all of which have astounding effects; and Mandala Meditation for Reincarnation, which brings you closer to the state of the Buddha.

Lastly, Part III provides visual explanations of Methods for Practicing Deep Concentration and Meditation, for practicing more advanced meditation techniques; Flower Meditation Method II, the second stage of the basis of meditation; How to Practice the Four Routes, for practicing recollection and concentration simultaneously; Ajna Meditation Method, which uses a magical Kundalini pearl to secrete hormones at will; Crystal Dragon God Cleansing and Meditation Method, which uses a crystal to invigorate the depths of our consciousness; and lastly Ragaraja Secret Mandala Meditation Method.

It is considered that, properly speaking, these methods of training that I have taught should not be committed to paper or video. This is because training of the chakras in the brain can be

dangerous depending on how it is practiced, and caution is required. These videos have been produced in a way that makes these difficult training methods easy to understand so that you can practice them safely, and so I want you to thoroughly master these meditation methods.

Part III of *Practicing Meditation for Reincarnation* brings to a provisional conclusion the texts of the videos on Meditation for Reincarnation. In these videos I have explained it for serious practitioners as far as possible, but there is still much more to Meditation for Reincarnation. It has great depth to it.

I encourage those who wish to advance to higher levels of training, and even those who do not, to first practice thoroughly the contents of these texts and videos and then to receive further training from me or from a disciple who has been directly instructed by me.

Lastly, I wish to mention the most important mental preparation for practicing this.

The Buddha Shakyamuni, who taught how to escape reincarnation, is described as having been fully endowed with all virtues or merits. There is no way to become a Buddha without merit. This is patently obvious. Someone who is ill-fated and meritless succeeds in nothing.

This also applies to Meditation for Reincarnation. In one respect, Meditation for Reincarnation is a "technique." But one cannot succeed in Meditation for Reincarnation by means of "technique" alone. Someone who does not have sufficient "merit" and "fortune" to endure the practice of Meditation for Reincarnation will be unable to accomplish it however much he or she may practice.

In fact, they will be unable to master the techniques themselves. Obstacles will invariably arise, and they will be unable

Prologue   13

to continue practicing. Or else they will become exhausted, fall by the way, and abandon their practice.

You must accumulate as much merit as possible to improve yourself.

If you practice Meditation for Reincarnation with such an attitude, you will most certainly be able to enjoy a better future and an ideal next life.

Auspicious day, June 2016
Seiyu Kiriyama

Methods for Practicing
Deep Concentration
and Meditation

Shamatha and Vipashyana

First of all, meditation is training that uses the mind, and there are two ways of using one's mind. We could say they are the two abilities of the mind. The first is concentration, or the ability to concentrate. The other, conversely, is the ability to expand. Both of these abilities are ways to use one's mind.

In Sanskrit, the original language of Kundalini yoga, concentration is shamatha and expansion is vipashyana. The mind's abilities are divided into these two abilities.

These two Sanskrit words shamatha and vipashyana were translated into Chinese by Chinese monks many years ago very simply and clearly as "stopping" (shamatha) and "visualizing" (vipashyana). Zhiyi, the founder of the Tiantai tradition of Chinese Buddhism, subsequently systematized the practice of shamatha and vipashyana. The translations "stopping" and "visualizing" are truly wonderful translations.

In other words, stopping means to continually concentrate in your mind, to focus on one thing, to concentrate your mind on it. In the beginning, you see a flower as a whole. When focusing on it – concentrating closely – you focus on it and don't move from the flower's core. This is the true power of concentration. The ability to concentrate is very important among the ways of using the mind. First, you must develop a good ability to concentrate.

However, just concentrating is not enough. Next, you must visualize. This is the ability to visualize things in your mind, to see images in your mind – to be able to create images of things in your mind, to actually see things in your mind.

Stopping is, so to speak, concentrating and fixating on an image in your mind. Visualizing is to realize that object. This is

expressed in esoteric Buddhism as contemplation. Sooner or later, all of you will have to learn how to contemplate. This includes visualizing a picture or an image.

However, simply creating an image isn't enough. Are you with me? Vipashyana does not just mean creating an image. It is realizing an image.

Therefore, we must both visualize and realize. We must visualize something, and then look at it closely. Not just look at it, observe it. Observe it closely. Then concentrate your mind on what you have observed.

These are not separate things, but the same thing.

Methods for Visualizing All Sorts of Objects in Your Mind
Visualize all sorts of objects in your mind. This doesn't mean just creating simple images. Visualize things necessary for your studies, and then concentrate your mind on them. Then focus on them and keep the visualization stationary. Don't let it move. Concentrate on it and bring that visualization into your mind.

In reality, you don't just bring it into your mind. There is something more advanced than that, but you won't understand it at this stage of your training. Right now, it will be difficult enough for you to just focus. You won't be able to do anything more.

You will most likely repeatedly struggle with focusing on the object and preventing it from moving around. At first, practice and learn how to focus properly.

One problem is what sort of image you should create. What should you visualize? A guru will decide for you. You should visualize this or that. This depends on how much training you have had.

At first, you will be told to visualize the same items. As time passes, this will change in accordance with your age, your constitution, and various other factors.

Therefore, if told to visualize something round, some people may visualize a dumpling. Others may visualize the moon. Another person will visualize a round tray. Someone may even visualize a person with a snub nose and chuckle. It depends on each person. So, for this reason a guru will teach you each and every specific object to visualize.

In the beginning, everyone will visualize the same thing. And then everyone will be told to concentrate their mind on that object.

By practicing these two abilities, you will gradually get better at them. Then you can use your ability to concentrate to move the cells in your own body.

For example, you can concentrate your mind on your stomach. With this concentration, you could secrete gastric fluid for example. Or by visualizing an umeboshi (dried plum), you could produce saliva when you are thirsty.

Many years ago Cao Cao, a famous general in China's Three Kingdoms period, was marching with his troops. They had run out of water, and everyone was thirsty and exhausted.

They then saw some trees in the distance, and Cao Cao said to his troops, "It's a grove of plum trees. Let's head towards it. The trees should have ripe plums. If we go there and eat the plums, we will no longer be thirsty."

Well, just hearing the word "plum" produced saliva in everyone's mouth. They were able to quench their thirst just by hearing the word "plum." When they arrived, there weren't any plum trees. There was just a bunch of bushes. However, it

provided temporary relief for the soldiers' thirst.

This is how we can visualize things.

Training to Enhance the Ability to Concentrate

The next thing you can do to increase your powers of concentration is to stop looking at things vaguely. Always observe things closely. You should look, not see.

But just staring isn't enough. Observe closely. If you make it a habit, you will not just see things, and they will make a lasting impression on your mind.

Just by looking at something like this, or glancing at that, or seeing this here or there, you will be able to observe and recreate it in your mind. You must become able to do this.

During my training when I was young, I practiced many things to develop my visual skills and my ability to concentrate and visualize. For example, I would look outside when my eyes became tired while reading a book.

When doing so, I would see a power line and some birds perched on it. I would look at this quickly and immediately close my eyes. I would then recreate the scene and count the remaining birds in my mind. I could see those birds ... one, two, three, four, five, six birds. And over here ... one, two birds ... a total of sixteen birds.

Anyone can do this with just a little training. It gets complicated when there are 35 or 36 birds. You mustn't think about how many birds there are up there. Don't think, just observe exactly what you see.

So, quickly look at these sliding doors and count how many there are ... one, two, three, four, five, six, seven.

It's the same for anything. Quickly look at a person's face.

There's a nose in the center, and above it are two eyes.

Developing such powers of observation will lead to being able to concentrate and visualize. Look at a book, but don't read it. Look like this, and then close your eyes. Then recall the printed words.

I often did this sort of training in my younger days. So, you too can train like this at any time.

While riding the train on the way to work or school, hold onto a strap like this and a building will appear in the distance. Quickly close your eyes and count the number of windows it has. The number of windows on this side like this, and the number of windows on that side like this.

You mustn't think. Don't think. Look quickly, close your eyes, and count from the image remaining in your mind.

You will see a big difference after doing this for just one month. This technique is perfect for cheating during a test. Have a quick look and observe everything. However, it doesn't do any good if you observe the wrong answers. Therefore, don't use the ability to steal another person's answers, but to look at your own notes.

Training to Control the Mind
Now, this is most important. How can we develop our minds to work in this way? As I just said, one way is to just observe with your eyes and count. There is another way, which basically involves being able to make your mind do whatever you want it to.

This other method is breathing. We breathe. All humans breathe, don't we? Breath and our minds are connected. They are very closely related. Are you following me? Our minds and

breathing have a very close relationship.

Your mind doesn't function readily the way you want it to. But you can control your breathing to a certain extent. Therefore, if a secret connection exists between this and that, you will be able to control your mind by controlling your breathing.

Trying to control only the mind is a rather difficult task. As I just said, one way is to increase your observation skills when quickly looking at something and being able to count the number of things you see after just a glance, but this is not the fundamental issue.

So what should you do in order to fundamentally control your mind and make it function as you please? You should first try to control your mind using the secret connection between the mind and breathing. This is because, while it may be difficult to control the mind, it's not so difficult to control your breathing.

I think you understand. Breathe deeply. You can exhale and inhale, right? In the beginning, though, it's difficult to concentrate.

However, stop breathing deeply and take quicker breaths and hold them. This you can do, right? It all starts from this.

This is how you can begin to control your mind.

Strive, Sure of Success

As a frame of mind you should maintain from now on as you study meditation methods hard and learn the method for gaining a good memory and intelligence, I will talk about one way to prepare yourself.

Work hard and be confident that you will succeed. By doing this, you will gain all sorts of wisdom to achieve success.

If you think of yourself negatively and think that you can't do something, your wisdom will probably remain untapped. Can a person make progress if he or she thinks negatively and prevents any advancement?

By thinking that you will be successful no matter what, you will be able to call upon wisdom to ensure success. If you do this, you will definitely succeed.

You should also never complain, grumble, criticize others, and speak ill of others behind their backs. This lowers your morals. A person's face when speaking ill or complaining about others looks mean. Anyone who consistently speaks that way will take on a mean face.

Human beings should be cheerful and not speak ill of others. Everyone likes a person with a cheerful disposition.

People don't help others unless they have good character. You must be kind. If you are not friendly in the eyes of others, you will not be able to achieve anything of significance. Successful entrepreneurs are always regarded as kind people and good partners and attract persons who want to help.

The opposite is hurting an unfavorable person's chances of success. This is not right. Not even the greatest person can succeed if he is disliked and ignored by others. Even a commonplace businessperson respected by others who help him out will certainly be successful.

A cheerful mind is necessary to have a pleasant personality. You must never say anything negative, speak ill of others, or think gloomily. Always be cheery and bright and think fairly. If you do this, your face will change in a month's time. You must strive for this.

Above all, your subconscious will become extremely aware and always move you in the right direction and provide you with good clues. And you will become such a person.

Therefore, don't speak negatively from today, and continue meditating with the confidence that you will definitely succeed.

Flower Meditation
Method II

Flower Meditation Method II

Let's begin the flower meditation.

One of the main purposes of meditation is to possess a pure, beautiful mind like a flower. Thus, we begin with a flower.

What we are going to do now is meditation in order to recollect and concentrate simultaneously.

Please sit comfortably in the half-lotus position. Anyone who cannot do this may sit in a chair.

First, exhale slowly.

Then, inhale slowly.

Breathe without making any sound.

Visualize a White Rose

Once your breathing and mind have become one, close your eyes and visualize a single white rose blossom.

Put that white rose in the center of your mind. Then, stare at the white rose. Not the notion of a white rose, but create in your mind an actual white rose.

Visualize a Red Rose

Next, visualize a red rose while keeping the white rose intact in your mind. Not the notion of a red rose, but create in your mind an actual red rose.

Clearly visualize the redness of that rose. Not the notion of red, but perceive the color red just as it is without forgetting about the white rose in the center of your mind.

Visualize a White Chrysanthemum

Next, visualize a white chrysanthemum blossom while keeping

26   Practicing Meditation for Reincarnation (Part III)

the white rose intact in your mind. You may erase the red rose. Create in your mind an actual white chrysanthemum, not just the notion of a large-blossomed white chrysanthemum. Clearly visualize the whiteness of the large-blossomed chrysanthemum. Not the notion of white, but perceive in your mind the color white as it is without forgetting about the white rose in the center of your mind.

Visualize an Orange Tulip
Next, visualize an orange tulip while keeping the white rose intact in your mind.

Visualize a Yellow Daisy
Next, visualize a yellow daisy while keeping the white rose intact in your mind.

Visualize a Pink Peony
Next, visualize a pink peony while keeping the white rose intact in your mind.

Visualize a Blue Iris
Next, visualize a blue iris while keeping the white rose intact in your mind.

Finally, you may erase the blue iris and stop meditating.

Although we just kept the white rose in the center, it's all right to change the fixed flower whenever necessary. The most important point is not to conceptualize, but to distinctly visualize the shape and color of each flower.

This method of meditation enables us to fix our mind on a single item, and at the same time successively visualize things related to that item. By doing these two things – recollecting and concentrating – at the same time, we can invigorate our brain activity.

How to Practice the Four Routes

In order to clearly meditate and concentrate, you must devise ways to develop the central object of your focus. Let's now do the four routes training for exercising the mind, which is necessary to achieve this.

How to Practice the Four Routes

First, as a way to prepare for the training, breathe peacefully. That is, try to breathe as naturally as possible without counting.

Then, fix on a specific object and carefully position it in the center of your mind. Without becoming detached from it, put that object on the four routes for exercising the mind and allow yourself to think freely.

Release any tension. Quiet the mind while maintaining your powers of concentration. This is the most important thing.

The Group Route

First, we have the Group Route.

Here, with a ranch as our setting, let's use a cow, something found on a farm, as the object with which to train. We will then visualize animals in the same group as a cow.

Cow

Slowly close your eyes and visualize a cow. Not the notion of a cow, but an actual cow.

While keeping this cow in the center of your thoughts, think of another animal in the same group.

Sheep

You could, for example, visualize a sheep. Clearly visualize a sheep while persistently keeping the cow intact in your thoughts. Not the notion of a sheep, but an actual sheep.

Horse

Next, visualize a horse. You may erase the sheep. Clearly visualize a horse while persistently keeping the cow intact in your thoughts.

Dog

Next, visualize a dog. You may erase the horse. Clearly visualize a dog while persistently keeping the cow intact in your thoughts.

In this same way, continue to visualize animals that resemble a cow.

The Parts Route

Next is the second training method, the Parts Route.

Visualize the different parts that comprise the body of a cow. Slowly close your eyes and visualize a cow once again. Think of the different parts of a cow's body while keeping the cow intact in your thoughts.

Cow's Ear

You could, for example, visualize a cow's ear. Clearly visualize a cow's ear while persistently keeping the cow intact in your thoughts. Not the notion of a cow's ear, but an actual cow's ear. Think of this as an ear, a part of a cow's body.

Cow's Nose

Next, visualize a cow's nose. You may erase the cow's ear. Clearly visualize a cow's nose, while persistently keeping the cow intact in your thoughts. Not the notion of a cow's nose, but an actual cow's nose.

Cow's Hoof

Next is a cow's hoof. You may erase the cow's nose. Clearly visualize a cow's hoof while persistently keeping the cow intact in your thoughts. Not the notion of a cow's hoof, but an actual cow's hoof.

In this same way, continue to visualize different parts that make up the body of a cow.

The Quality Route

The third type of training is the Quality Route.

Visualize the various qualities of a cow, such as its color, shape, size, and behavior.

Slowly close your eyes and visualize a cow once again. Think of a cow's movements while keeping the cow intact in your thoughts. Clearly visualize a cow's movements while persistently keeping the cow intact in your thoughts.

Turtle

Its slow movements are just like those of a turtle. Not the notion of a turtle, but visualize an actual turtle. Think of this as a turtle, whose slow movements resemble those of a cow.

Tractor

Next, think of how big a cow is. Something that resembles a cow's size, strength, and imposing air… a tractor. You may erase the turtle.

Clearly visualize a tractor while persistently keeping the cow intact in your thoughts. Not the notion of a tractor, but visualize an actual tractor. Think of this as a tractor, which is similar in size to a cow.

Go Stones

Next, think of a cow's color. What resembles the black and white of a dairy cow… a stone used to play go and other games. You may erase the tractor.

Clearly visualize go stones while persistently keeping the cow intact in your thoughts. Not the notion of go stones, but visualize actual go stones. Think of this as go stones, which is the same color as a cow.

In this same way, continue to visualize different qualities that resemble the color, shape, size, and behavior of a cow.

The Experience Route

The fourth type of training is the Experience Route.

You are now going to recollect various things associated with a cow, things that your experiences have impressed upon your mind.

Slowly close your eyes and visualize a cow once again. Think of a cow that was especially memorable while persistently keeping the cow intact in your thoughts.

Recollect as many things as you can that are associated with a cow.

Milk

Now, visualize a bottle of milk. Clearly visualize a bottle of milk, which comes from a cow, while persistently keeping the cow intact in your thoughts. Not the notion of a bottle of milk, but an actual bottle of milk. Think of this as a bottle of milk that has come from a cow.

Barn

Next, think of a barn, the place where cows live on a farm. You may erase the bottle of milk.

Clearly visualize a barn while persistently keeping the cow intact in your thoughts. Not the notion of a barn, but an actual barn. Think of this as a cowshed, where a cow lives on a farm.

Hay

Next, think of hay, something that a cow eats on a farm. You may erase the barn.

Clearly visualize the hay while persistently keeping the cow intact in your thoughts. Not the notion of hay, but actual hay. Think of this as hay, what a cow eats on a farm.

In this same way, continue to visualize from your varied personal experiences things connected to a cow that are especially memorable.

The benefits of these training methods are actually too many to measure. They can help you find direction and leave

34   Practicing Meditation for Reincarnation (Part III)

behind aimless wandering and other destructive habits, and give you the continued ability to concentrate on one thing for an extended period of time.

Setting a single focus for your mind and letting your thoughts and imagination run freely are essential for invigorating your subconscious. With further training, you should be able to realize how to utilize the depths of your consciouness.

Try to do them everyday without fail, even for just a short time.

Ajna Meditation
Method

The Ajna Meditation Method is a form of meditation that uses a magical Kundalini pearl to secrete and release necessary hormones as you require them. Those hormones will magically give you amazing powers.

Let's now see how to awaken the Ajna chakra

Ajna Meditation Method
Please sit comfortably, assuming either the lotus position or half-lotus position. Anyone who is unable to do so may sit in a chair.

Those familiar with the Breath of Fire should do it first.

Then breathe using the long exhalation and inhalation method for about two minutes.

Next, do the long exhalation method for about five minutes.

Those familiar with the reverse breathing method should do it here. However, women who are or may be pregnant should refrain from the reverse breathing method.

Then practice visualization. That is, think about what you are going to do and concentrate.

Put the Kundalini pearl you received from the instructor into your mouth.

Place the pearl in the "gum intersection."

Then move the pearl from the gum intersection to the tip of your tongue.

Then put it into the chakra prana route from under your tongue.

In rhythm with your long exhalations, gradually move the pearl downward.

From the "fluid receptacle" to the "chest center."

From the chest center to the "spirit gate."

Then, from the spirit gate slowly move it to the "ocean of

qi" in the case of men, or to the "origin of the pass" in the case of women.

The pearl should arrive at the ocean of qi or the origin of the pass while you breathe ten to fifteen times with the long exhalation method.

Once the pearl reaches the ocean of qi or the origin of the pass, it will have grown about twice in size and will gradually start to radiate light.

In this state, breathe five to ten times with the long exhalation method.

The pearl will gradually radiate less and return to its original size.

Soon, the pearl will begin to ascend.

Then, after breathing ten to fifteen times, the pearl will return to the gum intersection.

Once the pearl has returned to the gum intersection, it will then enter the Control Channel and continue to ascend.

It will then pass by the "extremity of the mouth," the "water trough," and the "white crevice" to the "courtyard of the spirit."

When the pearl reaches a point between "in front of the crown" and the "crown"(Sahasrara chakra), it will then enter the brain and move towards its center.

Soon, the pearl will reach the pituitary gland in the center of the brain and stop at the Ajna chakra.

The pearl, having stopped at the Ajna chakra, will have grown about twice in size and will gradually start to radiate light.

At this time, you should maintain a respiration rate that feels the most comfortable.

Soon the pearl will gradually radiate less and return to its original size.

In tandem with your breathing, the pearl will retrace its

movement along the chakra prana route and return to the gum intersection.

When the pearl has returned to the gum intersection, breathe about ten times with the long exhalation method.

Relax your breathing.

Then stand up slowly.

Crystal Dragon God Cleansing and Meditation Method

This method of meditation uses a crystal ball to invigorate the depths of our consciousness.

First, take out a crystal ball. A clear, natural crystal ball is ideal.

We are going to concentrate on the center of the ball.

When staring into the center of the crystal ball, you will see a lot of fog.

After calming down and then staring into the ball, you will soon be able to see the head of a dragon god. It is important that you become able to clearly see its figure.

It will take three days before you will be able to see its head and body within the fog.

You must contemplate, observe it well, and learn how to meditate.

Cleansing Meditation Method

We will start with meditation that cleanses both the mind and the body.

Water rained down by the dragon god will wash away all impurities and anything unpleasant from both the mind and the body and free them from the source of all illness.

Place a clear crystal ball in front of you.

Stare at it and soon changes will begin to happen.

A single cloud will suddenly start to form in a perfectly blue sky.

Then, a gust of wind will blow.

All of a sudden, the sky will become covered with black clouds.

Then, an even stronger wind will blow fiercely.

Envision a golden dragon in the center of the black clouds and concentrate on it in the center of your mind.

You can see the dragon in the crystal ball.

The golden dragon uses its god-given power to cause a windstorm.

It then starts to rain heavily.

You feel on your head the heavy rain coming down like a waterfall.

This is as if you were meditating while sitting under a waterfall.

The heavy rain completely rids your body and mind of all impurities and unpleasantness.

It washes away the source of all illness.

With these thoughts in your mind, recite the Heart Sutra five times.

Next, think about and pray for an invigorated body and mind completely rid of all impurities and unpleasantness.

Then, recite the Cundi Mantra five times:
On sharei shurei juntei sowaka. (× 5)

Lastly, say the nine-syllable mantra prayer three times:
Rin pyo to sha kai chin retsu zai zen ei!

Try to meditate once a day for about fifteen minutes.

By doing this purifying meditation every day, you will be physically invigorated throughout the day and be, moreover, protected by the dragon god.

Ragaraja
Secret Mandala
Meditation Method

1. Visualize a Vast Sky

Visualize a vast boundless expanse.

It's an expansive cosmic space far beyond our solar system and the Milky Way.

You are in the center of this space.

2. Agni

The letter "ran" 𑖨𑖽 appears in front your eyes.

    The letter "ran" 𑖨𑖽 turns into Agni, the god of fire.

    It emits a giant flame.

    The giant flame turns into a holy fire and spreads throughout the boundless expanse.

3. Dragon God Kulika

The dragon god Kulika appears within the giant flames of the holy fire.

Kulika then transforms into Acala, one of the Five Great Wisdom Kings – the Immovable One.

You and the holy fire become a single entity.

Nomaku sanmanda bazaradan kan

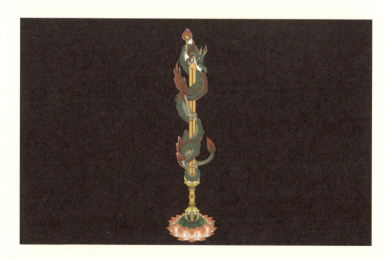

4. Trailokyavijaya

The letter "un" 𑖮 appears inside the flames.

The letter "un" 𑖮 turns into Trailokyavijaya, one of the Five Great Widsom Kings – the Conqueror of the Three Worlds.

It emits giant flames.

Trailokyavijaya's flames shine upon your mind.

They purify and free you from foolishness, greed, and anger—the three major mental afflictions that poison the minds of humans.

On sonba nisonba un bazara un hatta

Ragaraja Secret Mandala Meditation Method

5. Chakraratna

A Chakraratna, a wheel-shaped treasure possessed by the ideal ruler, appears inside the flames.

> The Chakraratna is enshrined in your umbilical ring.
> The giant flames envelop your body.

The Chakraratna then moves to your forehead.

It emits a giant flame and burns away all worldly desires that induce physical actions, namely, destructive habits.

The Chakraratna then moves to your throat.
It emits a giant flame and burns away all worldly desires that induce what we say, namely, malicious speech.

The Chakraratna then moves to your chest.

It emits a giant flame and burns away all worldly desires that induce our thoughts, namely, negative feelings.

You are purified and free from the three mental afflictions that poison the actions of body, speech, and mind.

6. Aparajita

Aparajita appears inside the giant flames.

The light Aparajita emits completely destroys all misfortune, difficulties, and bad luck.

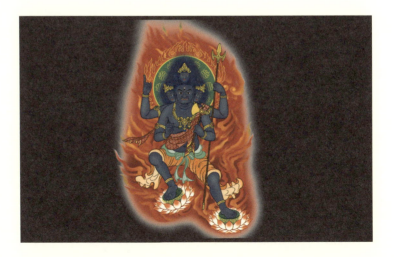

7. Wish-Fulfilling Banner

A wish-fulfilling banner appears inside the giant flames of the holy fire.

It emits rays of light from the wish-fulfilling jewel on top of the banner.

The rays begin to shine on you.

You then take in the rays of light and begin emitting them.

8. Sacred Relics of the Buddha

The letter "baku" appears inside the rays of light.

It emits golden rays of light.

The letter "baku" turns into the sacred relics of the Buddha.

The sacred relics of the Buddha, shining brightly, emit great rays of light into the vast expanse.

Your entire body emits rays of light and you and the sacred relics of the Buddha become a single entity.

9. Ragaraja

The letter "un" appears in the great rays of light.
    The letter "un" turns into Ragaraja.
    The letters of the mantra appear around Ragaraja.

    On makaragya bazoroshunisha bazarasatoba
    jaku un ban koku

Ragaraja Secret Mandala Meditation Method

10. Contemplation of Dependent Arising

Ragaraja and the letters of the mantra emit great rays of light as bright as the sun.

You are purified by the rays of light from Ragaraja shining on everything connected with you.

The rays return and shine on you again, changing everything connected with you into good fortune.

You are freed from all misfortune.

You are surrounded with good fortune, which will answer all your wishes and desires.

11. Twelve Gods

The twelve gods appear around you.
>They protect you from all calamities and misfortune.

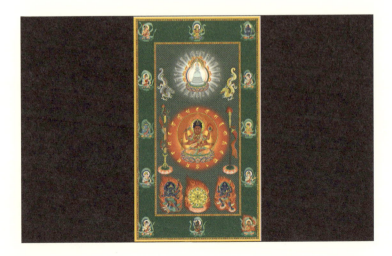

Concluding the Meditation

When your meditation is over, first release your mind from the meditation.

Clearly tell your mind the following: "I will now finish the meditation."

Next, open your mouth and audibly exhale qi three times.

Place your palms together in prayer.

Slowly swing your upper body back and forth to the left and to the right, four or five times.

Rub your hands together and place them over your eyes.

Then open your eyes wide and slowly look around you.

Rub your lower limbs, firmly place both feet on the floor, and stand up.

Lastly, facing your seat, put your palms together in gratitude and depart.

About the Author

Seiyu Kiriyama

Founder of Agon Shu Buddhist Association

Professor Emeritus, Peking University

Professor Emeritus, Beijing Foreign Studies University

Professor Emeritus, Zhongshan University

Professor Emeritus, National Buddhist Seminary of China (Buddhist College)

Professor Emeritus and Honorary Doctor of Philosophy, National University
of Mongolia

Honorary Doctor of Philosophy, Mongolian Academy of Sciences

Visiting Professor and Honorary Dean, Nyingmapa Tibetan Buddhist College

Honorary Doctor of Journalism and Mass Communication, Thammasat
University

Member of Board of Directors, University of San Francisco

Honorary SOAS Fellow, University of London

Honorary High Priest, Siam Nikaya Order of Sri Lankan Buddhism

Title of Highest Clerical Rank in Tibetan and Myanmarese Buddhism

Dharma lineage and full proficiency in the secret dharmas of Bhutanese
Buddhism; conferred title of 'Ngawang Gyaltshen' (Protector of Buddhist
Teachings Who Preaches Royal Sermons)

Director, International Qigong Research Center (Beijing)

Honorary Member, Dutch Treat Club (New York City)

Honorary Ninth *Dan*, Nihon Ki'in (Japan Go Association)

Honorary Vice Chairman, Zhongguo Weiqi Xiehui (Chinese Go Association)

Seiyu Kiriyama has written 68 books, including *Agon Buddhism as the Source of Shamatha (Tranquility) and Vipashyana (Insight); The Varieties of Karma; 21st Century: The Age of Sophia; You Have Been Here Before: Reincarnation; The Wisdom of the Goma Fire Ceremony; The Marvel of Spiritual Transformation and Sacred Buddhist Fire Ceremony for World Peace 2001; Practicing Meditation for Reincarnation, Parts I & II.*

Agon Shu Office Addresses

Main Temple
Shakazan Daibodai-ji
Omine-cho, Yamashina-ku, Kyoto, JAPAN

Kanto Main Office
Agon Shu Kanto Betsuin
4-14-15 Mita, Minato-ku, Tokyo 108-8318, JAPAN
Tel: 81-3-3769-1931

Kansai Main Office
Agon Shu Kansai So-hombu
Jingumichi Agaru, Sanjodori, Higashiyama-ku,
Kyoto 605-0031, JAPAN
Tel: 81-75-761-1141

Europe Branch Office
Agon Shu UK
First Floor, 31-33 Bondway,
London SW8 1SJ, England UK
Tel: 44-20-7587-5179

Canada Branch Office–Toronto Office
Agon Shu Canada Buddhist Association
Suite 205, 55 Eglinton Avenue East,
Toronto, Ontario M4P 1G8, CANADA
Tel: 1-416-922-1272

Brazil Branch Office
Associação Budista Agon Shu
Rua Dr. Nogueira Martins, 247 Saúde-São Paulo, BRAZIL
CEP: 04143-020
Tel: 55-11-3876-8812

Taiwan Main Dojo
Agon Shu Taiwan Honzan Dojo
1F., No. 27-6, Sec. 2, Zhongshang N. Rd., Tamsui Dist.,
New Taipei City 251,
TAIWAN (ROC)
Tel: 886-2-2808-4601

Taichung Taiwan Dojo
Agon Shu Taichu Dojo
Rm. B, 2F., No. 447, Sec. 3,
Wenxin Rd., Beitun Dist.,
Taichung City 406,
TAIWAN (ROC)
Tel: 886-4-2298-3380

Kaohsiung Taiwan Dojo
Agon Shu Takao Dojo
Rm. 1, 13F., No. 80, Minzu 1st. Rd.,
Sanmin Dist., Kaohsiung City 807,
TAIWAN (ROC)
Tel: 886-7-380-1562

連絡先——阿含宗に関するご質問・お問い合わせは左記まで

● 阿含宗本山・釈迦山大菩提寺　京都市山科区北花山大峰町

関東別院　〒108-8318 東京都港区三田四—一四—一五　☎(〇三)三七六九—一九三一

関西総本部　〒605-0031 京都市東山区三条通り神宮道上ル　☎(〇七五)七六一—一一四一

北海道本部　〒004-0053 札幌市厚別区厚別中央三条三丁目　☎(〇一一)八九二—九八九一

東北本部　〒984-0051 仙台市若林区新寺一—三一—一　☎(〇二二)二九六—五五七一

東海本部　〒460-0017 名古屋市中区松原三—一三—二五　☎(〇五二)三三四—五五五〇

北陸本部　〒920-0902 金沢市尾張町二—一一—二二　☎(〇七六)二三四—二六六六

九州本部　〒812-0041 福岡市博多区吉塚五—六—三五　☎(〇九二)六一一—六九〇一

大阪道場　〒531-0072 大阪市北区豊崎三—九—七　いずみビル一階　☎(〇六)六三七六—二七二五

神戸道場　〒651-0084 神戸市中央区磯辺通り二—一—一二　☎(〇七八)二三一—五一五二

広島道場　〒733-0002 広島市西区楠木町一—一三—二六　☎(〇八二)二九三—一六〇〇

横浜道場　〒231-0012 横浜市中区相生町四—七五　JTB・YN馬車道ビル五・六階　☎(〇四五)六五〇—二〇五一

沖縄道場　〒900-0031 那覇市若狭一—一〇—九　☎(〇九八)八六三—八七四三

● インターネットで阿含宗を紹介——阿含宗ホームページ　http://www.agon.org/

桐山靖雄（きりやま・せいゆう）

阿含宗開祖、中国・国立北京大学名誉教授、中国・国立北京外国語大学名誉教授、中国・国立中山大学名誉教授、中国・国立佛学院〔仏教大学〕名誉教授、モンゴル国立大学学術名誉教授、名誉哲学博士、モンゴル科学アカデミー名誉哲学博士、チベット仏教ニンマ派仏教大学名誉学長・客員教授、タイ王国・国立タマサート大学ジャーナリズム・マスコミュニケーション学名誉博士、サンフランシスコ大学終身名誉理事、ロンドン大学SOAS名誉フェロー、スリランカ仏教シャム派名誉大僧正、チベット仏教界・ミャンマー仏教界から最高の僧位・法号を授与、ブータン仏教界から法脈相承・秘法皆伝 法号「ンガワン・ゲルツェン〔王者の説法をする仏法守護者〕」を授与、中国国際気功研究中心会長（北京）、ダッチ・トゥリートクラブ名誉会員（ニューヨーク）、日本棋院名誉九段、中国棋院名誉副主席。二〇一六年、入滅。

主たる著書『密教・超能力の秘密』『密教・超能力のカリキュラム』『密教占星術Ⅰ・Ⅱ』『説法六十心1・2』『チャンネルをまわせ』『密教誕生』『人間改造の原理と方法』『阿含密教いま』『守護霊を持て』『統・守護霊を持て』『龍神が翔ぶ』『霊障を解く』『一九九九年カルマと霊障からの脱出』『輪廻する葦』『間脳思考』『心のしおり』『愛のために智恵を智恵のために愛を』『末世成仏本尊経講義』『守護霊の系譜』『一九九九年地球壊滅』『守護仏の奇蹟』『求聞持聡明法秘伝』『さあ、やるぞかならず勝つ①〜⑫』『仏陀の法』『守護霊が持てる冥徳供養』『密教占星入門』『人は輪廻転生するか』『君は誰れの輪廻転生か』『般若心経瞑想法』『一九九九年七の月が来る』『オウム真理教と阿含宗』『阿含仏教・超能力の秘密』『脳と心の革命瞑想』『阿含仏教・超奇蹟の秘密』『社会科学としての阿含仏教』『止観』の源流としての阿含仏教『一九九九年七の月よ、さらば』『21世紀は智慧の時代』『THE WISDOM OF THE GOMA FIRE CEREMONY』『The Marvel of Spiritual Transformation』『ニューヨークより世界に向けて発信す『You Have Been Here Before:Reincarnation』『実践般若心経瞑想法』『変身の原理』『幸福への原理』『守護神を持て』『仏陀の真実の教えを説く上・中』『あなたの人生をナビゲーション』『輪廻転生瞑想法Ⅰ・Ⅱ・Ⅲ』『美しい人になる心のメッセージ』（以上平河出版社）、『アラディンの魔法のランプ』（阿含宗出版社）、『念力』『超脳思考をめざせ』（徳間書店）、『密教入門—求聞持聡明法の秘密』（角川選書）など。

瞑想を終える

瞑想が終わったら、まず、瞑想から心を解き放つ。

「これで瞑想を終わる。わが身、良縁に包まれ、一切の願望成就す」

と、心にはっきりといい聞かせる。

つぎに口を開いて、ふーっと気を、三回吐く。

合掌する。

上体をゆっくりと左右に四、五回振る。

手を摩擦して眼を覆い、つぎに眼を大きく見開いて、ゆっくりと周囲を見る。

下肢を摩擦して、両脚でしっかりと床を踏みしめて立ち上がる。

ついで座に合掌して去る。

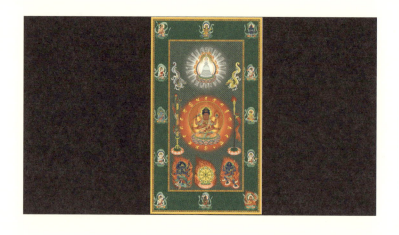

十一──神霊(しんれい)(十二天)

わが身の周囲に、十二天あらわる。
あらゆる天災、災難より守護し給う。

十一 縁起観

愛染明王と真言の字、日輪の如く大光明を放つ。

愛染明王の大光明、わが身を取り巻くあらゆる縁を照らし、
悪縁を浄めて輝く。

その光、還り来たって、わが身を照らし、すべての縁を良縁と化す。

悪縁すべて消滅して、良縁招来す。

わが身、良縁に包まれ、一切の願望成就す。

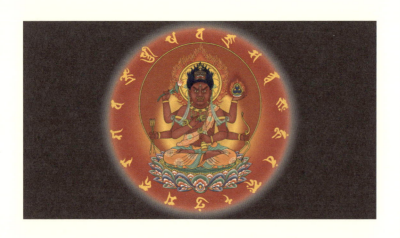

九 ── 愛染(あいぜん)明王

大光明の中に（ウーン）字あらわる。
変じて愛染明王となる。
周囲に真言の字があらわれ、
光明を放つ。

オーン・マカラギャ
バザロウシュニシャ
バザラサトバ
ジャク・ウン・バン・コク。

八―仏舎利尊

光明の中に 𑖀 (バク) 字あらわれ、
金色に輝く。
変じて仏舎利尊となる。
仏舎利尊、燦然(さんぜん)と輝き、
虚空中に大光明を放つ。
わが身、全身より光を放ち、
仏舎利尊と一体なり。

七―如意宝幢(にょいほうどう)

護摩の大火炎の中に、如意宝幢出現す。
頂の如意宝珠より光明を放つ。
光明、わが身に照り映(ほ)ゆる。
わが身、光明を受けてしだいに光を放つ。

六――無能勝明王

火炎の中に、
無能勝明王あらわる。
この尊の火光、
一切の災難、障難を打ち砕く。

(真言口伝)

実践 輪廻転生瞑想法 Ⅲ

輪宝、自身の胸に安置せよ。
火炎を発して自身の意業を焼き尽くす。
身口意の三毒燃え尽きて清浄となる。

愛染明王秘密曼荼羅瞑想法

輪宝、自身の喉に安置せよ。
火炎を発して自身の口業を焼き尽くす。